So there's going to be
a **new baby**
in your family?

And you'll soon be
a **big brother** or **big sister**?

Here's a special book just for **you**
to help you welcome
your **new baby**.

Other
Marlor Press
Books
for Kids:

Kid's Vacation Diary

Kid's Squish Book

Lake Superior, Wow!

My Camp Book

Kid's Address & Writing Book

Kid's Book
to Welcome
A New Baby

A fun activity book
of things to do and to learn
for a big brother or big sister

BARBARA J. COLLMAN

Published by

MARLOR PRESS, INC.

KID'S BOOK

TO WELCOME

A NEW BABY

Revised edition

Published by Marlor Press Inc. All rights reserved.
No part of this book may be reproduced in any form
without written permission of Marlor Press Inc.

Illustrations by Marlin Bree

Distributed to the book trade by
Contemporary Books, Inc., Chicago

New edition September 1995.
Printed in the U.S.A

ISBN 0-943400-83-X

DISCLAIMER: This book is intended only as a book of general activity
for children. It does not replace specific instructions or guidelines
by a parent, counselor, physician or others directly concerned
with the child's welfare. Though the author and the publisher have
made best efforts to present helpful information, a parent or adult
should insure that the child will work at his or her own capacity and
that the activities will meet the adult's own guidelines and standards
for the child's welfare and safety. In any event, Marlor Press, Inc.
and the author are not responsible for safety, services,
behavior, damage, loss or injury of any kind.

MARLOR PRESS INC.

4304 Brigadoon Drive
Saint Paul, MN 55126

CONTENTS

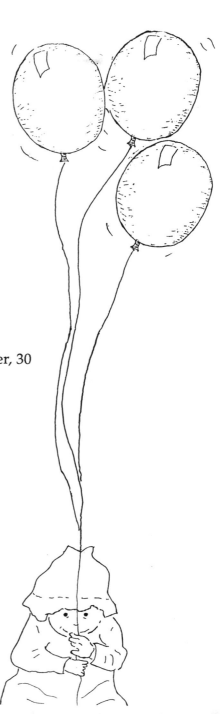

Part 4: WELCOMING THE NEW BABY

Part 5: WE GROW UP TOGETHER

K I D S !

How to have fun
with this book

Something exciting is happening in your family! Your mom and dad have told you that there will be a new baby in your family. You soon will have a baby brother or a baby sister! The Kid's Book to Welcome a New Baby will help you get ready to be a great big sister or big brother.

You can start today to read and do the activities in this book. You will learn many fun and important things about babies and how to keep them safe. Your mom and dad will be pleased with all you've learned. Remember that you will always need to get permission to play with your new little brother or sister.

A SPECIAL
NOTE
TO PARENTS

This book will help your child welcome the new baby. It will encourage interest in the baby and in being a big sister or brother. The activities are designed to open up family discussions and can be easily adapted to your child's age and abilities. Reading and working in this book together will let your child know that he or she is an important member of the family.

You can use **Part 1**, *All about me*; **Part 2**, *My family gets ready*; and **Part 3**, *All about babies*, from the time you choose to tell your child of the expected baby until her/his actual arrival. As soon as the new baby arrives, your child can go on to **Part 4**, *Welcoming the new baby*. The last section, **Part 5**, *We grow up together*, encourages your son or daughter to look forward to the days ahead and to learn more about what having a brother or sister really means.

Many pages are planned just for your child who is age two to five (approximately) to do with your help. Other more difficult activities may be appropriate for an older child of age six to twelve, but some activities might be modified for a younger child. For example, "Finding Out About Me," page 18, need not be followed as written, but you will sure-ly want to show and talk about the objects such as baby toys and pictures, as it reinforces the child's uniqueness. You may want to pick one or two activities from pages 41 and 42, "I Can Hardly Wait" to do together, but a younger child may not be interested or able to do them all. When drawing a picture, accept the child's ability level and don't ask for recognizable figures. For example, a drawing might look like a scribble but the addition of an adult label (given by the child and printed by the adult) of "My Family," will make it meaningful to everyone.

Young children are less able than older children to communicate verbally or to understand. They need to do more activities that require movement and motor skills but these abilities are also just beginning to develop. The following activities especially use manipulative skills and body movements but the child may need lots of adult help.

Page 13, Babies are Special; p. 26, My Booklet; p. 27, Treasure Box; p. 37, I remember; p. 40, Planning Ahead; p. 41, I Can Hardly Wait; p. 42, Touch Book and Zipper Up; p. 45, Everywhere We Go; p. 50, Doll Practice; p. 52, Still Growing; p. 54, Baby Faces; p. 56-61, Songs & Games; p. 64, Your Busyness; p. 73-75, Announcements; p. 81, Hand in Hand. Other activities that a younger child may enjoy are on pages 12, 13, 19, 21, 22, 24, 25, 26, 27, 32, 33, 34, 35, 37, 38, 39, 45, 46, 47, 48, 49, 50, 51, 53, 62, 66, 69, 70, 76, 77, 78, 82, 83, 86, 90, 91, 92, 99, 100, 109, 116, 120.

For a young child, you may want to fill in special pages so that the book will be a keepsake for the child as he/she grows older. For example, "Finding Out About Me" on page 18, or page 36, "My Helping Record," may be too difficult now but important to remember in the future.

If your child is age six and up, she/he will probably be able to carry out many activities and complete some of the written parts of the book without your help. You will want to allow your child some independence, of course, but stay involved. Remember, the book is intended to encourage family input and discussions so you will want to either guide the activities or do them with the child.

You play an important part in encouraging your child to take part in these preparation activities. For example, when your child helps by doing a family task, urge him/her to enter it on the "Helping Record," page 36.

TIPS FOR PARENTS

1. With any age child, but especially ages 2-5, choose the concepts you want to be sure the child knows and repeat them over and over. For example, just learning the words "in" or "on" are important to following directions. Use the concept over and over again, keeping your sentences short and simple. You might say "Put the paper on the table," and "Look, the book is on the chair."

2. Plan a quiet time every day when you can work on an activity or page from the book or just talk about the changes that are coming.

3. Be patient and ready to answer the same questions over and over. Not only is there a lot to understand, but there is time going by in which to forget the answers!

4. With a 2-5 child, pick a page or activity, read it aloud and talk about it. If there is a written portion, you might ask the child to tell you what to write.

5. With a 6-and-up child, agree on what page or activity he/she will be doing, read through it together and answer questions on how she/he might go about it. Some activities may require you steering the child in the right direction.

6. Use positive reinforcement. The child may not do an activity the way you would have done it but praise him or her for the creativity shown.

7. If your child is older and does not seem interested, try doing these as family activities. This may tempt her/him to do more, but demanding it is not a good idea.

8. There are many ways to expand the use of the book with older children. For example, a child might want to learn to play one of the songs he or she learned (Songs and Games to Share, page 56) on the piano.

PART 1

ALL
ABOUT
ME!

A special baby you know!
I was a baby, too!
Searching for clues about me
My great investigation
Finding out about me
Changing from baby to big kid
I like being bigger!
I am going to be a big brother or sister

A special baby <u>you</u> know!

Your mom and dad waited
for a special baby to be born.

Do you know who that was?

That baby was
<u>YOU</u>!

I was a baby, too!

My mom and dad were very happy
when **I** became part of the family.

⭐ **They named me:**

_____

Something special about my name is:

_____

_____

I was born on

Day_____ Month _____ Year_____

I was the: _____first child _____second child

_____third child or _____child in the family

Activity: Babies are special!

On a large piece of paper or pasteboard, glue pictures of babies
you cut from magazines. You will find many pictures of babies—
each one is a special member of a family.

Searching for clues about me

A good investigator:

☆ Starts with a plan ☆ Asks questions
☆ Knows who to ask ☆ Looks carefully

 ## Start with a plan:
THE **WHO**

WHO are the people who knew you
when you were a baby? Write their **names** below.
They are the best people to answer your questions
and help you find clues:

NAME _____

NAME _____

NAME _____

NAME _____

THE **WHATS**

WHAT **rooms** in your home might have **clues** or
objects that would tell you about you
when you were a baby?

ROOM _____

ROOM _____

_____

WHAT **places** might have
objects or **papers**
that have been hidden
away?

PLACE _____

PLACE _____

PLACE _____

WHAT papers or **objects**
do you think you might find?

_____

_____

_____

Now that your plan is ready, **get started!**

My great investigation

On the last two pages you made a plan to search for **clues** about **yourself** as a baby. Here you can write what you found out.

Date: _____

What I did: _____

_____

What I found out: _____

_____

Date: _____

What I did: _____

_____

What I found out: _____

_____

Date: _____

What I did: _____

_____

What I found out: _____

_____

Date: _____

What I did: _____

_____

What I found out: _____

_____

Date: _____

What I did: _____

_____

What I found out: _____

_____

_____

_____

Finding out about me

*Check which items
you found*

1._____Your Birth Certificate

2._____Your favorite toys

3._____Your baby pictures

4._____Some favorite clothes?

1. Did you find your Birth Certificate?

Here is some information you can find on it:

Length of my footprint: _____inches

My height: _____inches

My weight:_____pounds _____ounces

Time of birth:_____(a.m. or p.m.?)

Doctor's name:_____

Name of the hospital_____

2. Did you find your favorite baby toys?

Here is my list: _____

_____

_____

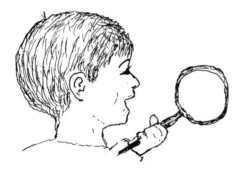

3. Did you find your baby pictures?

Here are some baby pictures you can look for:
(Check the ones you found.)

_____Me having my first bath

_____Me eating

_____Me with my whole family

_____Me at the hospital

_____Me in my first bed

_____Me sleeping

_____Me with mom

4. Did you find your baby clothes?

Here are some baby clothes I found:

_____

_____

Did you hear your birth day story?

Mom and Dad told me
the story of my birth day.
Their story:

_____

_____

_____

_____

_____

_____

Right after I was born, I had:

____some hair _____a little hair

_____no hair at all (poor me).

The first day home, I met

_____

_____

 ## My favorite song was...

_____

....especially if this person sang it to me:

_____

A toy I liked to sleep with was:

_____

My folks showed me off when they took me here:

_____

_____

This is a story about something funny I did:

My conclusions

I learned some things about me
I didn't know before

_____yes _____no

I knew a lot
about me before
my investigation

_____yes _____no

I was really surprised to find out:

_____

_____

I want to learn **even more** about
when I was a baby. Some things
I want to know more about are:

1. _____

2. _____

3. _____

4. _____

Changing from baby to big kid

Here's a picture taken of me when
I was a very, very new baby:

(Paste

your

BABY picture

here)

Here's a picture of me TODAY!

Wow! What a difference!

(Paste

your

BIG KID picture

here)

About me now:

I am_____years old. I am a _____boy _____girl.

I have _____colored eyes _____colored hair.

I am this tall_____ And I weigh this much_____

I live with_____

A day in my life

Write about what you do on an average day. Include the names of friends, pets, places you go, such as preschool, the library, or day care. Tell things you like to do— like color or listen to music.

- -

- -

- -

- -

- -

- -

- -

Activity: My booklet

Make up a booklet about you right now. Put in pictures of favorite neighbors and friends, the place you live, the park you like to play in, your favorite toys...anything important in your life. (Hint: This can be a great gift for a distant grandparent or other relative.)

From **baby** to **bigger**

I have already grown so much!
These are things I **don't** do anymore (For example, you don't
wear diapers, suck on a pacifier, or drink from a bottle):

_____

_____

_____

_____

I've grown enough **to do** these things: (**Tell** what I want instead
of cry, run fast, help wash dishes, comb my hair, wash my hands,
eat a cookie, go to the circus, go fishing or take a pony ride):

_____

_____

_____

I know what I like! These are things I **really like** (carrots, mashed
potatoes, chocolate chip cookies, or a teddy bear):

_____

_____

Activity: Treasure Box

Make a Treasure Box to keep your important things in. Get a shoebox
or any box with a lid. Cover the box and the lid with paper you like
or aluminum foil. Write on the outside: (your name's) Treasure Box.
Decorate the box with stickers or drawings. Look for some
favorite things to keep in it.

I like being bigger!

I'm blasting off
to being a big kid!
Here's a countdown
of my experiences:

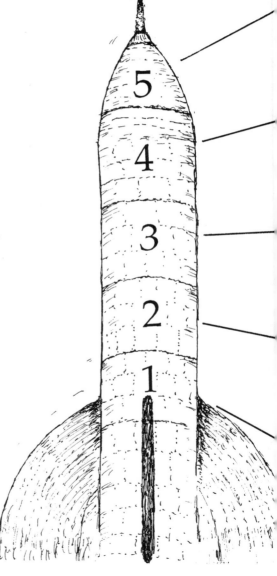

5 **Big kid things I have learned to do:**
(Tie my shoes? Ride a bike? Get Dressed? Other?)

My list: _____

_____

4 **Special places I have been:**
((A zoo? Circus? Play group?)

_____

_____

3 **Special things I am allowed to do:**
(Take lessons? Sleep over?)

_____

_____

2 **Special changes I would like when I become a big brother or big sister:** (More allowance? Bigger bed?)

_____

_____

1 **A special privilege I am hoping for in the future:**
(A later bedtime? A pet?}

_____

_____

I am going to be a BIG brother or sister

You are already a son or daughter, a grandson or grand-daughter, and maybe a little brother or sister. Now you will be a big brother or sister. Here's a place for you to write how you feel about having a new sister or brother, what you think it will be like, and what you think will be the best part of being the big brother or sister.

PART 2

MY FAMILY GETS READY

How many noses?
I am ready to help!
My helping record!
Helping with Dump Day!
Things to do to get ready!
I can hardly wait!

♥ Your family is waiting
for a special baby again!
You are happy and excited—
and busy getting ready!

How many noses?

♥ How many people
are in your family?_____

How many girls?_____

How many boys?_____

How many noses?_____

How many fingers?_____

How many hearts?_____

How many eyes?_____

How many toes?_____

Activities

♥ Collect pictures of families you know. Put them all together
in a group on a poster or in an album. Talk about
the family—are they cousins? Friends?

♥ On a large piece of paper or postcard, glue pictures of families
cut from magazines. Remember that there are lots of different
kinds of families.

♥ I AM
READY
TO HELP!

Your mom is busy doing a very important job.
She is taking care of the baby growing inside
her. She is working so hard at her special job
that she may need extra rest and she may also
need extra help.

BRILLIANT BRAIN: *Good to plan a* ***surprise*** *for mom.*

Your surprise: Fill a box, bag or basket with 14 small gifts (some for her, some for baby.) Tell her to open one every day starting about two weeks before the baby might come. For the baby, you can plan a surprise of a small stuffed toy, bib or booties. *Additional ideas:* You can give mom IOU's for washing dishes or watering the garden, or something else you can think of to help.

EAGLE EYES: To see when mom needs help. (Like tying her shoelaces.)

ESCALATOR VOICE: To go up loud for playing outside and to go down low when mom is resting.

GRIPPER HANDS: To carry a pillow for mom's back, slippers for her feet, and a glass of milk.

RACING FEET: To run and get whatever mom needs

MY
HELPING
RECORD

Here is a record of some ways I helped our family

Date   I helped by doing this:

- - - - - - -   -

- - - - - - -   -

- - - - - - -   -

- - - - - - -   -

- - - - - - -   -

- - - - - - -   -

- - - - - - -   -

- - - - - - -   -

- - - - - - -   -

- - - - - - -   -

- - - - - - -   -

Date	I helped by doing this:
- - - - - - -	- -
- - - - - - -	- -
- - - - - - -	- -
- - - - - - -	- -
- - - - - - -	- -
- - - - - - -	- -
- - - - - - -	- -
- - - - - - -	- -

Activities: "I remember" Game

Here is a game to practice following directions. A parent will play it
with you. You can see how well you can listen and do.

*Note to parent: Give your child a simple one-part direction to follow to help
with the baby. For example, you can say, "Please go to the crib." Then let your
child do the task. Did he or she remember? Be certain to follow up with lots of
praise. Or you can make the remembering a little more complex for an older
child by adding parts: "Please get the baby's teddy bear from the crib and
bring it here." Keep practicing. When the child is successful with two-part
directions, try three. You can do this over a period of months. Throughout,
the child will learn vocabulary and recognition of items associated with
the new sibling.*

This goes here—that goes there!

Here's another game. You can learn where things go to help the
family. Find out where to put toys, dirty clothes, and trash.

HELPING
WITH
DUMP DAY!

Your family may be planning a DUMP DAY!
That's a day to get out boxes of baby clothes,
blankets, bottles and other things the baby
will need. On Dump Day, you can help your
mom and dad find your old baby things and
help get them ready for the new baby.

FIND

the first toys the baby will play with,
such as:_____rattles _____soft stuffed animals
_____things that can be squeaked
_____or things that are made to be chewed

*Help wash them and put them in a special box
or basket. (Maybe you can decorate it.)*

FIND

the clothes the baby will wear
right away, such as:
_____pajamas with feet _____undershirts
_____or little socks

*Help wash and put them away
in the baby's own drawers.*

FIND OUT

what other things your family
must get ready, such as:
_____putting up the crib
_____getting out a car seat
_____cleaning a baby bathtub
_____or buying diapers

THINGS TO DO
TO GET READY

Help your mom and dad by making a list here.
Check each thing off when you have completed it:

Done

1 _____ ☐

2 _____ ☐

3 _____ ☐

4 _____ ☐

5 _____ ☐

6 _____ ☐

7 _____ ☐

8 _____ ☐

♥ Activities: Planning Ahead

Plan a walk that you will take with the baby. Put a doll in a stroller
and decide on a fun walk. When you see something pretty
or interesting, hear a bird or a train, show the baby!
Pretend a doll is the new brother or sister. Find out what it will be like
when the baby eats, gets a bath, gets changed, burps, etc.

I can hardly wait!

Five handy things to do while you wait

1 Make a special sign to put up on the day the baby comes home. You could draw a picture of your family on the sign and write, "Welcome to our Family."

After you know the baby's name, you could add:

"We Love you,_____

(add the baby's name).

2 Make a sign that says, SHHHHHH—BABY IS SLEEPING. Use cardboard or posterboard and decorate the sign. Put the sign in a place you will be certain to see it when you come in from outside. Turn it over until you need it.

3 Decorate a box or bag to hold some special "Mom and Me" and "Dad and Me" plans. Cut some slips of paper and write one activity you plan to do on each one. You might want, "Bake cookies with Mom," or "Take a walk with Dad." Put all the slips in the box or bag and mark the

outside with the instructions to draw one or two slips
every week.

4 Stitch, color or paint a picture for the baby's room.
(Check an art store for coloring posters.) Before you
frame it, sign your name and the date. Hang your gift in
the baby's room

5 Special gifts just for baby. Here are two projects to
make with a parent or a grandparent:

BABY BIB

Plan and make a bib for baby to use. Choose a pattern,
pick a design, and work together on a cloth or towel bib.

TOUCH BOOK

Find different materials that "feel" different—soft, smooth,
gritty, fluffy, etc. Put the pieces into a book, with or
without words.

♥ Activity: Zipper Up!

Get out some of baby's clothes, including sleepers and outerwear.
Practice buttoning, snapping, and using velcro. If your child is old
enough, show him or her how to protect the baby's skin while
zipping up clothing. If you have an educational toy that teaches
these skills, use it, or dress a doll in baby clothes for more practice.

PART 3

ALL
ABOUT
BABIES

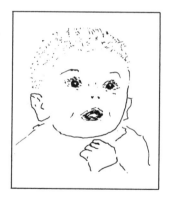

Baby watch   The zoo won't do!
Growing...growing!
May I?   Baby faces   Switches!
Songs and games to share!
Busy Days
I earned my Baby Ready Certificate

You will be a fun
big sister or **big brother**.

You will want to find out
the most
important things
about babies!

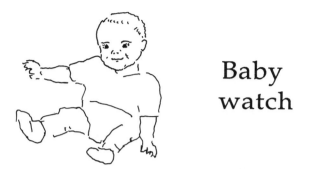

Baby watch

Count the babies you see in the store, on the street, on the bus, in the park, on the beach, or in the restaurant—wherever you go!
Try to guess the babies' ages. Are they under one year? Over one year?

Everywhere we go

Wherever you are, look for things related to babies and for items the baby might use. For example, at the grocery store, you can look at baby food. Maybe you can buy a jar and taste it. At a store, find the changing station and check to see if the shopping carts have infant seats.

The
zoo
won't
do!

Have you ever seen a baby animal
with its mother?
It's fun to watch how the mother
cares for her baby.

But the best way to learn
about taking care of a baby brother or sister
is to watch a human mother with her family.

The pictures here will show you
some animal mothers and babies.
You can visit a human mother and baby
or ask your mom and dad to help you learn
about baby care.

Then write what you found out!

A **mother kangaroo**

holds
her baby
like this

THE **ZOO** WON'T DO.
I learned **to hold** a baby
like this:

- -

- -

- -

- -

- -

- -

- -

A mother cat

carries
her baby
like this

THE **ZOO** WON'T DO!
I learned
to carry
a baby this way:

- -

- -

- -

- -

- -

- -

A baby **panda bear**

eats
this
way

THE **ZOO** WON'T DO.
I learned that a baby
eats this way:

**A baby opossum
sleeps
like this**

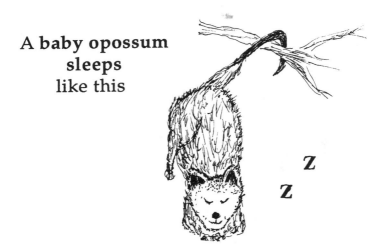

THE ZOO WON'T DO.
I learned that a baby **sleep**s like this:

Activity: Dolly practice
Ask your mom or dad to help you practice baby care
with a baby doll. You can learn lifting, carrying, holding,
burping, feeding, playing, sleeping positions,
dressing, washing, and lots more.

Growing... growing!

It may not seem like babies get bigger very fast,
but they are growing all the time.
While you are waiting for the baby,
try growing some flowers or plants.
What do flowers or plants need to grow?

What do babies need to grow?

...Still
growing

1 On a large piece of butcher paper or posterboard, trace
a doll or draw a realistic-sized baby. The adult can
draw in the facial features and the child can draw the hair
to match his or her baby pictures. Then get out one of the
child's baby outfits, one of the new ones, or just use a
picture of a baby outfit. Color in the clothes of the baby to
match.

2 Get a large piece of butcher paper or poster board.
Have the child lie down and trace his or her outline.
Help him make the facial features and pick the outfit he's
wearing or bring out a different one. Draw in the clothes
and let the child color or paint them.

3 Make a poster of the child using pictures of different
ages to show growth. Be sure to include a newborn
picture and a recent picture.

May I?

Mom and Dad need me
to follow a few rules:

___Pick up the baby when Mom or Dad say it's OK,
if I do it the way they tell me to do it.

___Touch the baby very gently with one finger.

___Give the baby food or drinks
made just for babies (not mine).

___Give the baby his or her own
special toys (not mine).

I realize I am strong, so I must be careful with baby.

OTHER RULES:

_____

_____

_____

_____

_____

_____

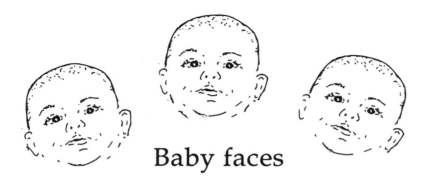

Baby faces

Here are some fun activities
to do with your hands:

1 Use fingerpainting paper or waxed paper, or a smooth surface. With a washable marker, draw a head and eyes, ears, nose, mouth, and hair. Now use oatmeal to paint a picture of a messy eater. You can add spaghetti hair, macaroni mouth, frosting cheeks, and candy eyes. Or, you can use fingerpaints.

2 Draw a picture of a baby face on paper. Then make it into a large-size puzzle. Cut it apart and put it back together.

3 You can also decorate round cookies with candies to make a baby's face.

♥ ♥ ♥ ♥ SWITCHES! ♥ ♥ ♥

Lots of fun **switches** may be going on soon. Will you
switch bedrooms with the new baby? Will you switch
from your usual seat in the car to a different place
when the baby's car seat goes in? When baby starts to
sit in a high chair, will you switch places at the table?
Here is a place to keep track of those **switches** you
see, both before and after the new baby comes:

Date   Switch!   **Why I like the switch:**

Songs and games to share

Babies love it when you **sing** to them and **play** little **games** with them. Ask your mom, dad, and grandparents to teach you their favorite songs and games for babies. You can also ask friends and neighbors or look in books for ideas.

Here are some of the **fun songs**
I learned to play with the baby:

Name of the song I learned: _

I learned it from: _

Words of the song: _

_ _

_ _

_ _

_ _

_ _

_ _

_ _

Name of the song I learned: _____

I learned it from: _____

Words of the song: _____

_____

_____

_____

_____

_____

_____

_____

_____

_____

_____

_____

_____

_____

_____

_____

_____

_____

Name of the song I learned: _____

I learned it from: _____

Words of the song: _____

_____

_____

_____

_____

_____

_____

_____

_____

_____

_____

_____

_____

_____

_____

_____

_____

Name of the song I learned: _ _ _ _ _ _ _ _ _ _ _ _ _ _ _ _ _ _ _

I learned it from: _

Words of the song: _

_ _

_ _

_ _

_ _

_ _

_ _

_ _

_ _

_ _

_ _

_ _

_ _

_ _

_ _

_ _

_ _

Fun games!

Do you know "This Little Piggy" and "Peek-A-Boo?"
Here are some of the games I learned
to play with the baby:

Name of game I learned: _

I learned it from: _

How to play the game: _

_ _

_ _

_ _

_ _

_ _

_ _

_ _

_ _

_ _

Name of game I learned: _____

I learned it from: _____

How to play the game: _____

_____

_____

_____

_____

_____

_____

_____

_____

_____

_____

_____

_____

_____

Dog-gone!

_____

_____

_____

BUSY DAYS

You are ready for the baby to come and are excited about enjoying your new sister or brother. Here are a few more things you should know about the busy days after the baby comes:

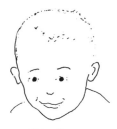

Baby
busy-ness

___The baby may need to go to the doctor's office or hospital for tests or check-ups. There are some special tests that every baby needs, and your parents want to be sure that the baby is healthy.

___The baby will sleep and eat, then sleep and eat, and then sleep and eat again. That's because sleeping and eating are just about all that newborn babies do.

___The baby will cry in between eating and sleeping. You might think at first that something is wrong or that your mom and dad are not trying hard enough, but the baby is probably only crying about as much as any other baby cries. And there are reasons for all that crying!

Mom & dad
busy-ness:

___Your mom will need extra rest. She is tired from her job of caring for the baby—she might have been awake taking care of the baby while you were asleep.

___Your dad may be able to stay home from work for a day or two after the baby arrives. He will want to help with the baby, but he will probably have some extra time to play with you, too!

Family
& friends
busy-ness

___People will come to visit. Your family and friends are just as excited about the new baby as you are! Some will come for a short visit; some may stay longer.

___People will call to talk—especially family members who do not live nearby.

Your busy-ness

You will start doing all the things you have learned—helping your family and helping with the baby.

You will have to pose for lots and lots of pictures!

You will think of things to do with all those pictures:

☆ Send some pictures to relatives who live far away.

☆ Make a scrapbook that will be just for pictures of you with your brother or sister.

☆ Ask your mom or dad to take a picture every three months; then glue it in your book.

☆ Make a frame with paper or craft materials. Put a picture of yourself in the frame and place it in the baby's room.

Other
busy-ness
for me

Make a list as you and your parents
think of ideas

1 _____

2 _____

3 _____

4 _____

5 _____

6 _____

7 _____

8 _____

9 _____

10 _____

I earned
my
Baby-Ready
Certificate

I am
Baby-Ready

♥ I practiced baby care

♥ I helped my family get ready

♥ I learned songs
and games for babies

♥ I promise to love and protect
the new baby in our family

_____

Signature

_____

Date

PART 4

WELCOMING
THE NEW
BABY!

I see the new baby!   Isn't that a cute baby?

I am happy to announce!   Do we look alike?

Was I that little?   Hand in hand

What can baby do?   Baby talk   Just call on me!

My family helping record   I talk to baby

What will baby do all day?   How baby learns

How we can play together   My activity record

What are they talking about?   The new baby is special

You have
a new baby sister
or baby brother!

You will want to get to know
the new baby
right away.

I see the new baby!

And here is my important record:

♥ Our family's **new baby** was born on:

_____
Day of the week

_____
Month   Day   Year

♥ The baby's full name is:

_____
First name

_____
Middle name

_____
Last name

♥ The baby weighs:

_____
       Pounds   Ounces

♥ That is (_____more) or (_____less) than I weighed when I was born.

I weighed:

_____
       Pounds   Ounces

♥ The baby's eyes are this color:

_____

♥ I first heard the news of baby's birth from this person:

_____

♥ When the baby came, I was at this location:

_____

♥ I was busy doing this:

_____

♥ I first saw the baby on this date:

_____

♥ At this location:

_____

♥ I first held the baby on this date:

_____

♥ At this location:

_____

♥ My feelings:

_____

_____

_____

How many noses now?

How many boys?_____ How many girls?_____
How many noses?_____ How many ears?_____
How many fingers?_____ How many toes?_____
How many eyes?_____
How many loving hearts?_____

**How many people
are in your family now?_____**

Isn't that
a cute baby?

Everybody loves babies! If you will listen carefully,
you will hear family and friends say many of the
same things over and over when they see the new
baby. Have you heard someone say these things?

"What an adorable baby!"   "The baby looks just like..."
"How tiny!" "You must be so proud!"

Your project is a fun one: Keep a list of the things
people say about your new baby. Write some of these
sayings below. Then, when he or she is older, you can
show them to your new brother or sister.

1 _____

2 _____

3 _____

4 _____

5 _____

I am happy to announce!

Now that the baby has arrived...

You can put up the
Welcome Home
sign you made

You can make and send or deliver
your own announcements to neighbors
or friends at school.

**Here are two ideas
on the next pages:**

Announcing
MY NEW
Baby Brother!

His name is BiLL
The date he was born: May 16, 1992
His weight is 8 pounds, 3 ounces

JiLL
His Proud Sister

A special
announcement

1/ Use a paper plate 2/ Draw a face with a marker
3/ Add hair color and eye color to match baby's
4/ Add a pink hairbow on the top for a girl. Add a blue
bow tie on the bottom for a boy.
5/ Write the announcement on the other side:

ANNOUNCING
my new
baby brother (or baby sister)

His or her name:_____

The date he or she was born:_____

His or her weight:_____

Signed_____
His proud sister (or brother)

Give your special announcement to your friends!

A baby-rattle announcement with a treat!

1/ Use two paper nut cups. 2/ Poke two holes in each cup. 3/ Thread a piece of curling ribbon through the holes. Tie the ribbon on the inside of the cups.
4/ Fill one cup with small candies. 5/ Write an announcement. Roll it up and put it inside:

I'm a Big Sister
(or a Big Brother)

The baby's name:_____

Date of birth:_____

Signed (your name)_____

                              Big Brother (or Big Sister)
6/ Glue the rims of the two cups together.
7/ Treat your friends to a baby rattle announcement.

♥ Do we look alike?

Here is one of the first pictures taken of the baby:

I think baby looks like me
because we have the same:

_____kind of nose   _____color of eyes

_____kind of hair   _____beautiful smile!

♥ Together:

(Baby's name)_____

and me on this date:_____

I am proud to have a baby _____.

(brother or sister)

(Baby's name)_____

Is lucky to have me for a big

_____ (sister or brother)

Was I ever that little?

You can discover the wonder
of a brand-new baby:

Look at the baby's feet and toes.
Are they as big as yours? ____Yes ____No

Count the toes.
How many are there?_____

Look at baby's footprint.
Does the baby have toenails? ____Yes ____No

How does baby's skin feel?
Is it smooth or rough? _____
What color is it?_____

Stroke the baby's skin gently.
Does the baby like to be touched?
____Yes ____No

Look at the baby's hands and fingers.
Have baby's fingernails been cut yet?
____Yes ____No

When I put my finger inside baby's hand,
this happens:

_____

_____

When I touch one of baby's cheeks, this happens:

_____

_____

Very gently touch the baby's hair.
Is it soft? ___Yes ___No

Ask your mom or dad why it is so important to be
careful of baby's head.

Look at the baby's lips.
Do baby's lips move even when he or she is not
eating? ___Yes ___No

Can you see bumps where baby's teeth will be?
___Yes ___No

Does the baby have eyelashes? ____Yes ____No

Are they long or short?_____

Does baby open his or her eyes very often?
____Yes ____No

What sounds does baby make?

_____

_____

_____

Does the baby cry softly_____ or loudly_____?

Does the baby make a sound when eating?
____Yes ____No

What sound?_____

When I gently touch one of baby's ears, this happens:

_____

When baby hears a sudden sound, this happens:

_____

When I gently touch the baby's lips, this happens:

_____

What fun babies are!

Hand in hand

Trace your hand below. Now trace the baby's hand
inside it with a different color. Write your names
inside the drawings.

What can baby do?

You may be surprised when you watch your new
brother or sister and see how many things
he or she can do already.

Sit right next to the baby. Read each line on the chart
on the next page and decide whether you can do it.
You can even try to do them right now!

If you can, put an X under "I can."

Then think about whether the baby can do the same
thing. Your mom or dad can help you decide and
remember what you have already seen baby do.

If baby can, put an X on the line. At the bottom of the
chart, you can add some things you think of.

	I CAN	**BABY CAN**
Hear noises	_____	_____
See	_____	_____
Taste	_____	_____
Smell	_____	_____
Feel	_____	_____
Talk	_____	_____
Cry	_____	_____
Breathe	_____	_____
Kick legs	_____	_____
Wave arms	_____	_____
Suck thumb	_____	_____
Blink	_____	_____
Understand	_____	_____
Hum	_____	_____
Sing	_____	_____
Whistle	_____	_____
Chew	_____	_____
Swallow	_____	_____
Walk	_____	_____
Crawl	_____	_____

Other things: _____   _____

_____   _____

_____   _____

BABY TALK

How does your baby brother or sister "talk" to you? When you need something, you can use words to tell your mom or dad, but what can the baby do?

When you hear the baby crying, you get to play a game. You can try to guess what the baby is telling you. Your mom and dad played this game when you were a baby, too—so they will probably guess faster.

Is the baby saying:

I'm hungry

I'm sleepy

I'm cold

I need to burp

I feel uncomfortable

I am too hot

Write your guesses on the next page:

M M M M M M E E E E E E E E E

What baby is saying

Date	My guess	Check here if you were right
- - - - - -	- - - - - - - - - - - - - - - - - - -	- - - - - - - -
- - - - - -	- - - - - - - - - - - - - - - - - - -	- - - - - - - -
- - - - - -	- - - - - - - - - - - - - - - - - - -	- - - - - - - -
- - - - - -	- - - - - - - - - - - - - - - - - - -	- - - - - - - -
- - - - - -	- - - - - - - - - - - - - - - - - - -	- - - - - - - -
- - - - - -	- - - - - - - - - - - - - - - - - - -	- - - - - - - -
- - - - - -	- - - - - - - - - - - - - - - - - - -	- - - - - - - -
- - - - - -	- - - - - - - - - - - - - - - - - - -	- - - - - - - -
- - - - - -	- - - - - - - - - - - - - - - - - - -	- - - - - - - -
- - - - - -	- - - - - - - - - - - - - - - - - - -	- - - - - - - -
- - - - - -	- - - - - - - - - - - - - - - - - - -	- - - - - - - -

**Can you guess
what baby
is telling you?**

Just call on me!

Here is a list of jobs
that I can do to help
the entire family

I can:

___ Pick up toys

___ Take messages

___ Bring in the mail or paper

___ Make lists

___ Fold laundry and put it away

___ Report on the baby

___ Go get whatever you need

I can do these things just for the baby:

___ Wind up a music box

___ Start a mobile

___ Take off shoes and socks

___ Talk or sing

___ Bring the bottle or pacifier

___ Wind up the baby swing

___ Just be around

More ideas
(from mom and dad)

_____

_____

_____

_____

_____

My family helping record

Here is a record of some ways I helped our family:

Date	I helped by
- - - - - - - - - -	- -
- - - - - - - - - -	- -
- - - - - - - - - -	- -
- - - - - - - - - -	- -
- - - - - - - - - -	- -
- - - - - - - - - -	- -
- - - - - - - - - -	- -
- - - - - - - - - -	- -
- - - - - - - - - -	- -
- - - - - - - - - -	- -
- - - - - - - - - -	- -
- - - - - - - - - -	- -
- - - - - - - - - -	- -

Date   I helped by

- - - - - - - - - -   -

- - - - - - - - - -   -

- - - - - - - - - -   -

- - - - - - - - - -   -

- - - - - - - - - -   -

- - - - - - - - - -   -

- - - - - - - - - -   -

- - - - - - - - - -   -

- - - - - - - - - -   -

- - - - - - - - - -   -

- - - - - - - - - -   -

- - - - - - - - - -   -

- - - - - - - - - -   -

- - - - - - - - - -   -

- - - - - - - - - -   - - - - - - - - - - - - - - - - - - -

- - - - - - - - - -   - - - - - - - - - - - - - - - - -

- - - - - - - - - -   - - - - - - - - - - - - - - - -

I talk to baby

When?

Anytime the baby is awake and listening to you.

Where?

 Sitting next to the baby.
Holding the baby.

Why?

So the baby can learn to talk when he or she is bigger.
So the baby will learn to know your voice.
So the baby will feel loved.

What?

You can tell the baby about things that are happening around him or her. Like this:

*"I just saw the puppy run by.
Did you see the puppy run by?
He was running fast!"*

Write something you might say here:

- -

- -

- -

- -

You can tell the baby about something you are showing him or her, like this:

"Here is your blue rattle. It has yellow flowers on it and it makes a noise when I shake it."

Write something you might say here:

- -

- -

- -

- -

You can talk about the baby.
Use the baby's name over and over
like this:

*"Look at Katy's long fingers!
They are pretty fingers, Katy.
I like to see Katy's pretty fingers."*

Write something you might say here:

_ _

_ _

_ _

_ _

_ _

**If you get tired of thinking
of things to talk about,
don't forget the baby
loves to hear
YOU
sing or hum
a song!**

What will baby do all day?

Here is a place to record one day of baby's life. It will be fun to tell someone who wasn't there what the baby did all day!

Baby did this:

♥ ♥ ♥ Some more things ♥ ♥ ♥
baby did all day: ♥ ♥ ♥

Today, the baby
had this many:

I see you, too!

___ Naps

___ Baths

___ Visitors

___ Changes of clothes

___ "Awake" times

___ Diaper changes

It won't be long until the baby starts staying awake more and more to watch what you are doing.

MY DAY

Here's how I spent one whole day:

_____

_____

_____

_____

_____

_____

_____

_____

_____

_____

_____

_____

How baby learns

How do you learn about the world? You see, hear, smell, touch, and taste to find out about things. You also can learn by asking other people about their favorite smells, sounds, tastes, and things to touch. You can guess about baby's favorite things, too.

♥ PERSON'S NAME

_____

His or her favorite:

Smell_____

Sound_____

Taste_____

Touch_____

♥ PERSON'S NAME

_____

His or her favorite:

Smell_____

Sound_____

Taste_____

Touch_____

♥ MY NAME

_____

My favorite:

Smell_____

Sound_____

Taste_____

Touch_____

I think
baby
would pick
these favorites:

♥   Smell

_____

♥   Sound

_____

♥   Taste

_____

♥   Touch

_____

How we can play together

Playground rules:

Make sure either mom or dad
tell you it's OK to play with baby.

Baby loves to see your face,
so stay very close
where he or she can see you.

If baby keeps watching you,
he or she is having fun.

Baby loves to play the same game
again and again.

If baby starts to cry, he or she may need
to rest a moment.

Make certain baby still wants to play.
He or she won't want to play
if it is time to eat or sleep.

Smile at the baby and give him or her
a gentle hug or pat.

You can play when the baby's in a seat,
swing, a lap, on a bed,
or on a blanket on the floor.

Only play games that are safe
for the baby.

Show the baby something bright and moving,
like a scarf, a pennant,
a child's mobile,
or anything else your parents approve.
Keep it close to the baby so he or she can see it.
Let the baby touch
what you are holding,
unless it could hurt the baby.

Show the baby a rattle and shake it.
Then move slowly around the room
while you
shake the rattle and say the baby's name.

Sing a song and clap
or do hand motions.
Move the baby's hands and feet
while you sing.
Say a rhyme and do motions
with your hands and with
the baby's hands.

**Play one of the baby games
you have learned.**

My activity record with BABY

Here is a list of some fun things baby and I did:

Date   What we did together:

- - - - - - - - -   -

- - - - - - - - -   -

- - - - - - - - -   -

- - - - - - - - -   -

- - - - - - - - -   -

- - - - - - - - -   -

- - - - - - - - -   -

- - - - - - - - -   -

- - - - - - - - -   - - - - - - - - - - - - - - - - - - -

- - - - - - - - -   - - - - - - - - - - - - - - - - - Dog-gone!

- - - - - - - - -   - - - - - - - - - - - - - - - - -

Date   **What we did together:**

----------   ----------------------------

----------   ----------------------------

----------   ----------------------------

----------   ----------------------------

----------   ----------------------------

----------   ----------------------------

----------   ----------------------------

----------   ----------------------------

----------   ----------------------------

----------   ----------------------------

----------   ----------------------------

----------   ----------------------------

----------   ----------------------------

----------   ----------------------------

----------   ----------------------------

----------   ----------------------------

Activity
Look back at the plans you made to do with baby.
Have you done them yet?

What are they talking about?

Have you heard words that you don't know?
They are probably words about babies and baby
things. You can write down the words here
and ask an adult what they mean.

Words I don't know: **What the words mean:**

_____   _____

_____   _____

_____   _____

_____   _____

_____   _____

_____   _____

_____   _____

_____   _____

_____   _____

Words I don't know:	What the words mean:
- - - - - - - - - - - - - - -	- - - - - - - - - - - - - - - - - - - -
- - - - - - - - - - - - - - -	- - - - - - - - - - - - - - - - - - - -
- - - - - - - - - - - - - - -	- - - - - - - - - - - - - - - - - - - -
- - - - - - - - - - - - - - -	- - - - - - - - - - - - - - - - - - - -
- - - - - - - - - - - - - - -	- - - - - - - - - - - - - - - - - - - -
- - - - - - - - - - - - - - -	- - - - - - - - - - - - - - - - - - - -
- - - - - - - - - - - - - - -	- - - - - - - - - - - - - - - - - - - -
- - - - - - - - - - - - - - -	- - - - - - - - - - - - - - - - - - - -
- - - - - - - - - - - - - - -	- - - - - - - - - - - - - - - - - - - -
- - - - - - - - - - - - - - -	- - - - - - - - - - - - - - - - - - - -
- - - - - - - - - - - - - - -	- - - - - - - - - - - - - - - - - - - -

Have you heard these words?

Pediatrician

formula

gums

What they mean:

A *pediatrician* is a doctor just for babies and kids.

Formula is a special baby milk.

Gums are part of the mouth where baby's teeth grow (and so do yours.)

The new baby is SPECIAL

Today my new

baby_____
(sister - brother)

is _____days old.
(number)

It seems like baby and I
have had our pictures taken
at least

_____times

So far my favorite thing to do with baby is

_____

I like helping by

_____

_____

I asked everyone in the family to tell something about the baby in only ONE WORD.

Here is what they told me:

Mom:

_____

Dad:

_____

Others:

_____

_____

And here is what I think
is the
best word
that tells about baby:

_____

PART 5

WE
GROW UP
TOGETHER!

Teaching baby
I am older, baby is younger
Do you want to be...   Growing up special
Growing up friends!
Other brothers and sisters
Baby's firsts!   Baby's learning record
I love you

Your new baby brother or sister
is growing and learning quickly.
You will see how much fun
you can have together.

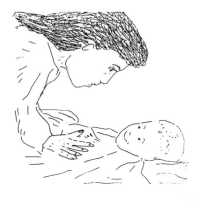

How can you tell
if the baby is learning?

You may see that the baby stays awake
more during the day. The baby may stop
crying more quickly when he or she
is picked up or fed. When you talk,
the baby
may make sounds back at you.

Teaching baby

Make a list of things you will help teach the baby when he or she is old enough. Here are some ideas: how to blow a kiss, how to count to ten, and animal sounds.

1 _____

2 _____

3 _____

4 _____

5 _____

6 _____

7 _____

8 _____

9 _____

10 _____

11 _____

12 _____

13 _____

14 _____

I am older, baby is younger

Have you been wondering how old you will be when your baby brother or sister has his or her first birthday? Here is a chart that is fun to do and that will show you your age and the baby's age for the next five years. On the first line, beside *Me*, put your age right now. Finish the chart with your mom's or dad's help. When you read across each line you can see the baby's age and your age at the same time.

Baby	Me
Newborn	_____
1/2 year	_____
1 year	_____
1 1/2 year	_____
2 years	_____
2 1/2 years	_____
3 years	_____
3 1/2 years	_____
4 years	_____
4 1/2 years	_____
5 years	_____

Do you want to be...

Big brother and big sisters have chances to do different jobs as they grow up.

Maybe you will be:

---a baby sitter

---a playmate

---a teacher

---a cheerleader
(encourage baby's learning)

---a helper

---a leader
(put your seatbelt on)

Your ideas on other jobs you can do:

_____

_____

_____

Growing up special

As you and your new sister or brother get bigger and bigger, what do you think will be special about being kids together in the same family? Will it be special because you can plan surprises for mom and dad together? Or because you will have someone to play with, even on vacation? Here's a place to write what you think:

I think growing up with a new sister or brother will be special because:

_ _

_ _

_ _

_ _

_ _

_ _

_ _

_ _

 # Growing up friends!

Most moms and dads wish that their children will be good friends. They may have ideas about how brothers and sister get along. Ask your mom and dad what they wish for their kids as they grow up. You can write what they say here.

DAD

MOM

Other brothers and sisters

Ask one of your parents and a brother or a sister to remember something about their growing up together. Some might remember trips they made together, going to a school, or sharing a room.

♥ **Name** _____

His or her favorite remembrance about **growing up**:

_____

A favorite **memory** when they played together (playing a game, swimming, sledding):

_____

What he or she said was the **best thing** about having a sister or brother:

_____

♥ **Name** _____

His or her favorite remembrance about **growing up**:

_____

A favorite **memory** when they played together
(playing a game, swimming, sledding):

_____

What he or she said was the **best thing** about having
a sister or brother:

_____

♥ **Name** _____

His or her favorite remembrance about **growing up**:

_____

A favorite **memory** when they played together
(playing a game, swimming, sledding):

_____

What he or she said was the **best thing** about having
a sister or brother:

_____

Baby's Firsts!

You probably can't remember the first time you ate
ice cream. But your parents can tell you about the
surprised look on your face when you felt the cold
and tasted the sweetness. You will have the fun of
seeing your new baby brother or sister find out about
the world. Be watching for Baby's Firsts and record
them here. Have fun —but remember some
may not happen right away.

Baby's first ice cream   Date_____

What happened:_____

_____

Baby's first popsicle   Date_____

What happened:_____

_____

Baby's first snow angel   Date_____

What happened:_____

_____

Baby's first clapping   Date_____

What happened:_____

_____

Baby's first somersault   Date_____

What happened:_____

_____

Baby twirls around   Date_____

What happened:_____

_____

Baby's first trip down a slide   Date_____

What happened:_____

_____

**Baby's first motorboat
sound with mouth**   Date_____

What happened:_____

_____

Baby sees soap bubbles   Date_____

What happened:_____

_____

Baby's first trike ride   Date_____

What happened:_____

_____

**Baby's first time
to say MY NAME**   Date_____

What happened:_____

_____

_____

Baby's learning record

These are some of the important things baby has learned already:

Date	☆	Baby learned
– – – – – – – – – – – –		– –
– – – – – – – – – – – –		– –
– – – – – – – – – – – –		– –
– – – – – – – – – – – –		– –
– – – – – – – – – – – –		– –
– – – – – – – – – – – –		– –
– – – – – – – – – – – –		– –
– – – – – – – – – – – –		– –
– – – – – – – – – – – –		– –
– – – – – – – – – – – –		– –
– – – – – – – – – – – –		– –
– – – – – – – – – – – –		– –

I LOVE YOU

A special letter
to baby

Dear_____
              (baby's name)

♡ It was a special day for all of us
    when you joined our family.
I have been helping take care of you
and I am excited that you will grow
          bigger and bigger
so I can play with you more and more.
When you are older, I will tell you
      about when you were a baby
and about the things we did together.
But mostly I will tell you how much
    we have always loved you.

Love,

My name_____

    Date_____